Your Money Matters

A Personal Finance Guide for Thriving in the UK

I0490598

RYAN STUBBS

DEDICATION

This book is for you, on your journey to financial stability and security. May it guide and empower you as you create the financial future you deserve.

CONTENTS

1
INTRODUCTION TO PERSONAL FINANCE

Welcome to the world of personal finance! This is the place where you can take control of your money, achieve your financial goals, and live the life you've always wanted. Whether you're just starting out or looking to improve your current situation, this chapter is the perfect starting point for anyone looking to dive into the exciting world of personal finance.

First things first, let's talk about why personal finance is so important. It's not just about managing your money, it's about managing your life. By taking control of your finances, you'll reduce stress, achieve your goals, and live a life that you're proud of. When you're in control of your money, you have the power to make decisions about how to use it and where to allocate your resources. This is a big deal, and it's the foundation of financial success and stability.

So, how do you get started with personal finance? The first step is to set some financial goals. These goals can be short-term or long-term, and they should be specific, measurable, and achievable. Some common financial goals include saving for a down payment on a house, paying off debt, or building an emergency fund. Whatever your goals may be, make sure they're important to you and that you have a clear understanding of what you want to achieve and why.

Once you have your financial goals in place, it's time to start creating a budget. A budget is a powerful tool that helps you manage your money and reach your financial goals. By tracking your income and expenses, you'll be able to see where your money is going and make adjustments as needed. The budgeting process is simple, but it takes discipline and commitment. So, buckle up, because we're about to dive into the exciting world of budgeting!

To create a budget, start by listing your income from all sources, including your job, investments, and any other sources of income. Then, list all of your expenses, including housing, food, transportation, entertainment, and any other expenses. Subtract your expenses from your income, and voila! You'll see if you have a surplus or a deficit. If you have a deficit, don't worry. This is a common starting point for many people. Just look for ways to reduce your expenses, increase your income, or both.

So, what are income and expenses? These are the two main components of your budget, and understanding them is essential for managing your finances effectively. Your income is the money you earn from all sources, including your job, investments, and any other sources of income. Your expenses are the money you spend on housing, food, transportation, entertainment, and other expenses. By understanding your income and expenses, you'll be able to make informed decisions about how to allocate your resources and reach your financial goals.

Personal finance is the foundation of financial success and stability. By setting financial goals, creating a budget, and understanding your income and expenses, you can take control of your finances and live the life you've always wanted. This is just the beginning, so don't be afraid to dive in and get started on your personal finance journey. The road ahead may have some bumps, but with determination and commitment, you'll be well on your way to achieving your financial goals and living a life you're proud of.

2
BUILDING A STRONG FINANCIAL FOUNDATION IN THE UK

In this chapter, we'll explore the importance of building a strong financial foundation and provide practical advice for creating an emergency fund, paying off debt, and understanding and improving your credit score. By following these guidelines, you'll be setting yourself up for financial success and peace of mind.

I. Creating an Emergency Fund

An emergency fund is a crucial component of a strong financial foundation. It's a set amount of money that you set aside to cover unexpected expenses, such as a job loss, medical emergency, or car repair. Without an emergency fund, you may find yourself relying on high-interest credit cards or loans to cover these unexpected costs, which can quickly lead to debt and financial stress.

To start building an emergency fund, set a goal for the amount you want to have saved. A common recommendation is to have three to six months' worth of living expenses saved in your emergency fund. This may seem like a daunting amount, but you can start small and gradually increase your savings over time.

To build your emergency fund, consider setting up automatic savings from your paycheck or bank account. You can also reduce your expenses by cutting back on non-essential spending, such as dining out, entertainment, and shopping. Look for ways to save money on your monthly bills, such as negotiating with service providers for lower rates.

The benefits of having an emergency fund are numerous. You'll have peace of mind knowing that you have a safety net in case of unexpected expenses. You'll also be better prepared to handle financial emergencies, which can reduce stress and improve your overall well-being. With an emergency fund in place, you'll also be less likely to rely on high-interest debt to cover unexpected expenses.

II. Paying Off Debt

Debt can quickly spiral out of control if not managed properly, and it can take a significant toll on your financial well-being. Whether it's credit card debt, personal loans, or mortgage debt, paying off debt should be a top priority for anyone looking to build a strong financial foundation.

To start paying off debt, it's important to understand the types of debt you have and the interest rates you're paying. Create a list of all your debts and their interest rates, and prioritize paying off the debt with the highest interest rate first. This will help you save money on interest over time.

To pay off debt, you'll need to create a budget. Start by listing your monthly income and expenses, and look for ways to reduce your expenses. Consider cutting back on non-essential spending, such as dining out, entertainment, and shopping. You can also negotiate with service providers for lower rates on your monthly bills.

Another option for paying off debt is debt consolidation, which involves taking out a loan to pay off multiple debts. This can simplify your monthly payments and potentially lower your interest rate, making it easier to pay off your debt. However, it's important to carefully consider the terms of the loan and make sure it's the right option for you.

Paying off debt can have numerous benefits. You'll reduce your financial stress and free up money for other financial goals, such as saving for retirement or investing. You'll also improve your credit score as you make on-time payments and reduce your debt-to-income ratio. Additionally, paying off debt can help you sleep better at night and reduce stress, leading to improved overall well-being.

III. Understanding Credit Scores and How to Improve Them

Your credit score is an important factor that lenders and service providers use to determine your creditworthiness. A good credit score can open up doors for you, such as access to lower interest rates and more favorable terms on loans and credit cards. On the other hand, a low credit score can limit your options and make it more difficult to secure loans or favorable terms.

To understand your credit score, you can request a free credit report from one of the UK's three credit reference agencies: Equifax, Experian, or TransUnion. These reports will show you your credit history, including information about your credit accounts, payment history, and outstanding debts.

To improve your credit score, there are several steps you can take:

Make payments on time: Late or missed payments can have a negative impact on your credit score. Make sure you pay your bills on time, every time.

Reduce your credit utilization ratio: This is the amount of credit you're using compared to your credit limit. A high credit utilization ratio can indicate that you're overextended, which can negatively impact your credit score. To reduce your credit utilization ratio, consider paying off debt or asking for an increase in your credit limit.

Dispute errors on your credit report: If you find errors on your credit report, dispute them with the credit reference agency. They will investigate and, if necessary, make the necessary corrections.

Avoid applying for new credit unnecessarily: Every time you apply for credit, it shows up on your credit report and can lower your credit score. Avoid applying for credit unless you truly need it.

Keep old credit accounts open: The length of your credit history is a factor in determining your credit score. Keeping old credit accounts open, even if you're not using them, can help improve your credit score over time.

Improving your credit score can have numerous benefits. With a good credit score, you'll have access to lower interest rates and more favorable terms on loans and credit cards. You'll also have more options when it comes to borrowing money, making it easier to achieve your financial goals. Additionally, a good credit score can be a sign of financial responsibility and stability, which can be attractive to potential lenders, landlords, and employers.

Building a strong financial foundation is crucial for financial success and peace of mind. By creating an emergency fund, paying off debt, and understanding and improving your credit score, you'll be setting yourself up for a bright financial future. Remember to take small steps and be patient, as these changes don't happen overnight. But with consistency and dedication, you'll be on your way to a strong financial foundation in no time.

3
INVESTING FOR YOUR FUTURE

Investing is an important part of personal finance and can help you achieve your long-term financial goals, such as retirement or buying a home. It's important to understand the different types of investments and how they can help you reach your goals.

Different types of investments

Stocks: Stocks, also known as equities, are a type of investment that give you ownership in a company. When you own a stock, you're effectively buying a small piece of the company and are entitled to a share of the profits. Stocks can be bought and sold on stock exchanges and can provide a good return over the long-term, but they can also be volatile in the short-term.

Bonds: Bonds are a type of investment where you lend money to a company or government in exchange for a fixed rate of return. Bonds are generally considered less risky than stocks, but they also have lower returns.

Mutual funds and exchange-traded funds (ETFs): Mutual funds and ETFs are a type of investment that pools money from multiple investors to buy a diversified portfolio of stocks, bonds, or other assets. These types of investments can provide a convenient way to invest and can be less risky than investing in individual stocks or bonds.

The role of a financial advisor

A financial advisor can help you understand the different types of investments and develop a personalized investment strategy based on your goals, risk tolerance, and time horizon. They can also help you diversify your portfolio and make recommendations for how to manage your investments over time.

It's important to choose a financial advisor that you trust and who has your best interests in mind. You can check if a financial advisor is authorized to provide financial advice by checking the Financial Conduct Authority's (FCA) Register.

Understanding risk and diversification

Investing always involves some degree of risk, but you can manage that risk by diversifying your portfolio. Diversification means investing in a variety of different types of investments and spreading your money across different industries, countries, and asset classes. This can help reduce your overall risk, as a loss in one investment may be offset by gains in others.

Investing is an important part of personal finance and can help you achieve your long-term financial goals. By understanding the different types of investments, the role of a financial advisor, and the importance of diversification, you'll be able to make informed investment decisions and work towards a secure financial future. Remember, investing involves risk and it's important to consider your risk tolerance before making any investment decisions. It's always a good idea to seek the advice of a financial advisor before making any investment decisions.

4
RETIREMENT PLANNING

Retirement is a time in your life when you can finally relax, enjoy life, and live without the worry of having to go to work every day. However, in order to make this dream a reality, it's important to start planning for retirement early.

The importance of starting early

Starting early with your retirement planning has a number of benefits. Firstly, it gives your money more time to grow through investment returns. Secondly, the earlier you start, the less you need to save each month to reach your retirement goals. And finally, starting early gives you more time to adjust your plans if necessary, allowing you to make any necessary changes along the way.

Different types of retirement accounts

There are several types of retirement accounts available in the UK, each with its own set of rules and benefits. Some of the most popular types of retirement accounts include:

Personal pension: A personal pension is an individual pension plan that you can set up yourself. You can contribute to the pension each month, and the money is invested on your behalf.

Occupational pension: An occupational pension is a pension plan that is set up by your employer. Your employer will typically make contributions to the plan on your behalf, and you may also be able to make contributions yourself.

Self-Invested Personal Pension (SIPP): A SIPP is a type of personal pension that gives you more control over how your money is invested. With a SIPP, you can choose the investments that you want to make and can manage the investments yourself.

Understanding pensions and annuities

Pensions and annuities are two important concepts to understand when it comes to retirement planning. A pension is a type of retirement plan that is designed to provide you with an income in retirement. An annuity is a type of financial product that you can use to turn your pension savings into a guaranteed income for life.

When you reach retirement, you can use your pension savings to purchase an annuity. This means that you'll receive a guaranteed income each month for the rest of your life, regardless of how long you live.

Retirement planning is an important part of personal finance. By understanding the importance of starting early, the different types of retirement accounts available, and the concepts of pensions and annuities, you'll be able to make informed decisions about your retirement and work towards a secure financial future. Remember, it's never too early (or too late) to start planning for retirement, and it's always a good idea to seek the advice of a financial advisor if you need help.

5
MANAGING TAXATION

Taxation is a complex issue that affects everyone in the UK. Whether you're an employee, self-employed, or a business owner, it's important to understand the UK tax system and how it impacts your personal finances.

Understanding the UK tax system

The UK tax system is made up of a number of different taxes, including income tax, National Insurance, value added tax (VAT), and capital gains tax. Understanding the different taxes and how they work is the first step to managing your tax liability and making sure that you're paying the right amount of tax.

Income tax:

Income tax is a tax on your income, including your salary, wages, and any other forms of taxable income. The amount of income tax you pay depends on how much you earn and your personal circumstances, such as your age, marital status, and the number of children you have.

National Insurance:

National Insurance is a tax that you pay if you're employed or self-employed. The amount you pay depends on your earnings and your personal circumstances, and it helps to build up your entitlement to certain state benefits, such as the state pension.

Value Added Tax (VAT):

VAT is a tax that's applied to most goods and services in the UK. If you're a business owner, you'll need to register for VAT if your taxable turnover exceeds a certain threshold. If you're a consumer, you'll pay VAT on most goods and services you purchase.

Capital gains tax:

Capital gains tax is a tax on the profit you make when you sell an asset, such as shares or property. The amount of capital gains tax you pay depends on the profit you make and your personal circumstances, such as your tax bracket.

How to reduce your tax liability

There are several steps you can take to reduce your tax liability and make sure that you're paying the right amount of tax. Some of the ways to reduce your tax liability include:

Make use of tax allowances: There are several tax allowances available in the UK, including the personal allowance, which is the amount of income you can earn each year without paying tax. Make sure you're making use of all the tax allowances you're entitled to in order to reduce your tax bill.

Claim tax credits: Tax credits are designed to help people with low to moderate incomes, and they can provide a significant boost to your income. Make sure you're aware of the tax credits you're entitled to and claim them where possible.

Use tax-efficient investments: Certain investments, such as ISAs and SIPPs, are tax-efficient, which means that you can earn tax-free returns. Make sure you're making use of these investments to help reduce your tax bill.

Maximizing tax benefits and credits

In addition to reducing your tax liability, there are several ways to maximize the tax benefits and credits available to you in the UK. Some of the ways to do this include:

Make the most of ISAs: ISAs are tax-free savings accounts, and they're a great way to save for the future. Make sure you're using your ISA allowance each year to take advantage of the tax-free returns.

Use your pension to reduce your tax bill: Pensions are a tax-efficient way to save for retirement, and they can also help to reduce your tax bill. Make sure you're contributing to your pension each month to take advantage of the tax benefits.

Invest in tax-efficient funds: There are several tax-efficient funds available, which can help you to earn higher returns and reduce

6
PROTECTING YOUR ASSETS

One of the key aspects of personal finance is protecting your assets and securing your financial future. Insurance is an important tool that can help you do just that, providing a safety net in case of unexpected events. This chapter will help you understand the importance of insurance, the different types of insurance available in the UK, and how to choose the right coverage for your needs.

The Importance of Insurance

Insurance is a crucial aspect of personal finance, providing a safety net in case of unexpected events such as death, illness, or accidents. It can help you protect your income, assets, and family from financial hardship, allowing you to focus on recovery without worrying about the financial consequences.

Understanding Different Types of Insurance

There are several types of insurance available in the UK, each with its own set of features and benefits. Some of the most common types of insurance include life insurance, health insurance, car insurance, home insurance, and travel insurance.

Life Insurance: This type of insurance provides a lump sum payment to your beneficiaries in the event of your death. It can help protect your family from financial hardship and ensure that your dependents are taken care of in the future.

Health Insurance: This type of insurance covers the cost of medical treatment and hospitalization. It can help you manage the cost of healthcare expenses and ensure that you receive the best possible treatment.

Car Insurance: This type of insurance covers the cost of repairs or replacement of your car in the event of an accident, theft, or damage. It can help you protect one of your most valuable assets and ensure that you're not left with unexpected expenses.

Home Insurance: This type of insurance covers the cost of repairs or replacement of your home in the event of damage, theft, or natural disasters. It can help you protect your home and possessions from financial losses.

Travel Insurance: This type of insurance covers the cost of medical expenses, cancellations, and other unexpected events while traveling. It can help you protect your travels and ensure that you have peace of mind while on vacation.

Choosing the Right Coverage for Your Needs
With so many types of insurance available, it's important to choose the right coverage for your needs. Consider the following factors when choosing insurance coverage:

Your current financial situation: Take into account your current income, assets, and liabilities when choosing insurance coverage.

Your personal circumstances: Consider your age, health, and lifestyle when choosing insurance coverage.

Your future plans: Take into account your future goals and plans when choosing insurance coverage.

Your budget: Make sure that you choose a coverage that fits within your budget.

By taking the time to understand the different types of insurance available and choosing the right coverage for your needs, you can protect your assets and secure your financial future.

7
ESTATE PLANNING

Estate planning is a critical aspect of personal finance that is often overlooked. It involves creating a plan for what will happen to your assets and property after you pass away. Estate planning is important for everyone, regardless of your age or the size of your estate. It provides peace of mind that your loved ones will be taken care of and that your wishes will be honored after you are gone.

Understanding the Importance of a Will

A will is a legal document that outlines how you want your assets to be distributed after you pass away. It is the most basic form of estate planning and provides a roadmap for your loved ones to follow. A will is especially important if you have children, as it allows you to designate a guardian for them. Without a will, the distribution of your assets will be determined by the court, which could result in your assets being distributed in a way that you may not have intended.

Creating a Plan for Your Assets

Estate planning is not just about creating a will. It also involves considering how you want your assets to be distributed, and what you want to happen to your property after you pass away. This includes your bank accounts, investments, real estate, personal property, and any other assets you may have. A well-designed estate plan can help you minimize taxes, reduce the cost of probate, and avoid family disputes.

Designating a Power of Attorney

Designating a power of attorney is another important aspect of estate planning. This is a legal document that allows someone you trust to make decisions on your behalf if you become unable to do so. There are two types of power of attorney: general and limited. A general power of attorney gives the person you designate the authority to make any decisions you could make, while a limited power of attorney gives them the authority to make only specific decisions. Designating a power of attorney can provide peace of mind that your affairs will be handled in the way you want, even if you are unable to make decisions yourself.

Estate planning is a critical aspect of personal finance that is often overlooked. By understanding the importance of a will, creating a plan for your assets, and designating a power of attorney, you can ensure that your wishes are honored and your loved ones are taken care of after you are gone. Don't wait until it's too late to create an estate plan. Consult a financial advisor or estate planning attorney to help you get started today.

8
CONCLUSION

Congratulations, you've made it to the end of this book and have taken a big step towards gaining a comprehensive understanding of personal finance! In this chapter, we'll recap some of the key concepts you've learned, encourage you to continue growing your knowledge, and offer some final thoughts on creating financial stability and security in the UK.

Key Concepts:

Building a strong financial foundation: This involves creating an emergency fund, paying off debt, and understanding your credit score.

Investing for your future: Different types of investments, the role of a financial advisor, and the importance of understanding risk and diversification were covered.

Retirement planning: Starting early, understanding different types of retirement accounts, and pensions and annuities were all topics of discussion.

Managing taxation: We explored the UK tax system, ways to reduce your tax liability, and maximizing tax benefits and credits.

Protecting your assets: Insurance was discussed, including the importance of choosing the right coverage for your needs.

Estate planning: We emphasized the importance of creating a will and designating a power of attorney, among other topics.

We hope that you've found this book to be helpful and informative, but there's so much more to learn about personal finance! As you continue your journey, remember to stay curious and ask questions. Seek out resources and information from trusted sources, such as the UK government's financial guidance website, to keep your knowledge up-to-date.

Final thoughts on creating financial stability and security:

Financial stability and security are achievable goals, and it all starts with a solid understanding of personal finance. By following the advice in this book, you're well on your way to creating a brighter financial future for yourself and your loved ones. Whether you're just starting out or looking to take your financial knowledge to the next level, remember that every small step you take is a step towards a more secure future.

In conclusion, we hope this book has given you the confidence and knowledge you need to make informed decisions about your finances. Stay the course, stay disciplined, and you'll be well on your way to creating a secure financial future.

Thank you for reading!